THE HISTORY OF SPACE EXPLORATION

SPACE

PROBES

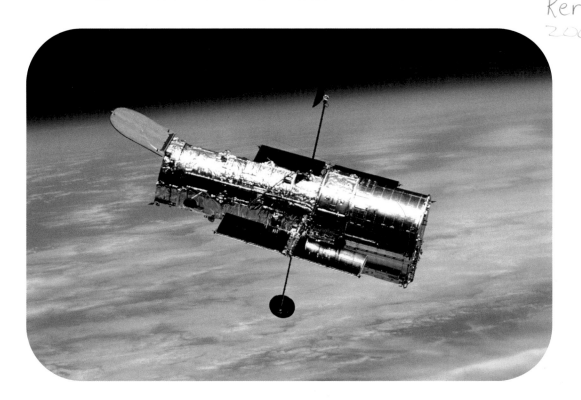

ROBIN KERROD

WORLD ALMANAC® LIBRARY

Please visit our web site at:
www.worldalmanaclibrary.com
For a free color catalog describing
World Almanac® Library's list of high-quality
books and multimedia programs, call
1-800-848-2928 (USA) or **1-800-387-3178
(Canada).** **World Almanac® Library's** fax:
(414) 332-3567.

Library of Congress Cataloging-in-Publication Data

Kerrod, Robin.
    Space probes / by Robin Kerrod.
        p. cm. — (The history of space exploration)
    Includes bibliographical references and index.
    ISBN 0-8368-5708-9 (lib. bdg.)
    ISBN 0-8368-5715-1 (softcover)
    1. Space probes—Juvenile literature.   I. Title.
II. Series.
TL795.3.K47   2004
629.43'5—dc22   2004048207

First published in 2005 by
World Almanac® Library
330 West Olive Street, Suite 100
Milwaukee, WI 53212 USA

Copyright © 2005 by World Almanac® Library.

Developed by White-Thomson Publishing Ltd
Editor: Veronica Ross
Designer: Gary Frost, Leishman Design
Picture researcher: Elaine Fuoco-Lang

World Almanac® Library editor: Carol Ryback
World Almanac® Library designer: Kami Koenig
World Almanac® Library art direction: Tammy West

Photo credits: top (t), bottom (b), left (l), right (r)
All images used with the permission of NASA except:
Novosti: 13. Spacecharts Photo Library: 4, 8, 12(t),
12(b), 14, 16, 17, 20(t), 23(t), 23b, 27, 30(b), 32, 33(t),
34, 35(t), 36, 37(t), 39, 41. Artwork by Peter Bull.

Printed in Canada

1 2 3 4 5 6 7 8 9 09 08 07 06 05 04

Cover image: Pioneer 10 *flying past Jupiter.*

Title page: The Hubble Space Telescope *in orbit in 2002.*

Contents page: Astronaut at work repairing the Hubble
Space Telescope.

▼ *Venus's volcanic landscape from the* Magellan
space probe.

CONTENTS

PROBING OUTER SPACE

It is January 2, 2004. After a five-year journey from Earth, a U.S. spacecraft named *Stardust* dives into the head of the Wild-2 ("*Vilt*-2") comet. It photographs the comet's icy core 146 miles (236 kilometers) away. More importantly, it collects samples of the dust particles streaming away from the core with a paddlelike device the size of a tennis racquet.

Leaving the comet behind, *Stardust* heads back toward Earth. On January 15, 2006, a capsule containing the dust will plunge through the atmosphere and be recovered. Scientists hope that this material—little altered for five billion years—will shed light on how our Solar System began and evolved.

Stardust is one of the deep-space probes now exploring our Solar System. Both the Soviet Union and the United States sent probes to explore the Moon and then the planets—almost as soon as they began launching satellites (the Soviet Union in 1957; the United States in 1958). A Soviet Union probe first reached the Moon successfully in 1959. *Luna 1* made a near flyby, *Luna 2* deliberately crash-landed, and *Luna 3* photographed the far side of the Moon for the first time.

The United States experienced little luck with its lunar spacecraft until the *Ranger 7* probe photographed the Moon's surface before crash-landing in 1964. Two years earlier, the U.S. launched the first successful deep-space probe, the *Mariner 2*. It flew past Venus and reported on planetary conditions.

Other probes since then studied and explored comets, asteroids, and all the planets (except Pluto) at close range. Probes revealed Mercury's baked, Moonlike surface; measured temperatures on Venus; indicated the presence of past oceans on Mars; captured images of erupting volcanoes on Jupiter's moon, Io; and showed rings around Uranus and Neptune. Unmanned spacecraft also photographed asteroids, analyzed the centers of comets, and even traveled beyond our Solar System into the far reaches of the Universe.

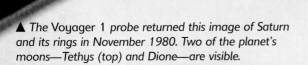

▲ The Voyager 1 probe returned this image of Saturn and its rings in November 1980. Two of the planet's moons—Tethys (top) and Dione—are visible.

CHAPTER ONE

THE SUN'S FAMILY

A star we call the Sun dominates our tiny corner of space. As the Sun hurtles through the Universe, it takes with it a "family" of planets, asteroids, and comets—which together form our Solar System. This is the family that space probes have explored.

The most important members of the Sun's family are the nine bodies we call planets. They circle the Sun at different distances from it. Earth is third in line from the Sun—after Mercury, the very closest to the Sun, and then Venus. Moving farther out after Earth and away from the Sun, in order, come Mars, Jupiter, Saturn, Uranus, Neptune, and Pluto.

The diagram below shows (roughly to scale) the planets' orbits, or paths, through space. Except for Pluto, all circle the Sun in much the same plane and direction—but they do not all rotate on their axis in the same direction.

PTOLEMY VERSUS COPERNICUS

Five hundred years ago, people thought that the Sun and its planets circled Earth. They believed Earth was the center of the Universe. The Earth-centered idea is often called the Ptolemaic system, for the last great astronomer of ancient times, Ptolemy (who lived about

▼ *The orbits of the planets in the Solar System. Earth is one of the four inner planets, which lie relatively close together in the center. The outer planets are wider apart. Most of the Solar System is just empty space.*

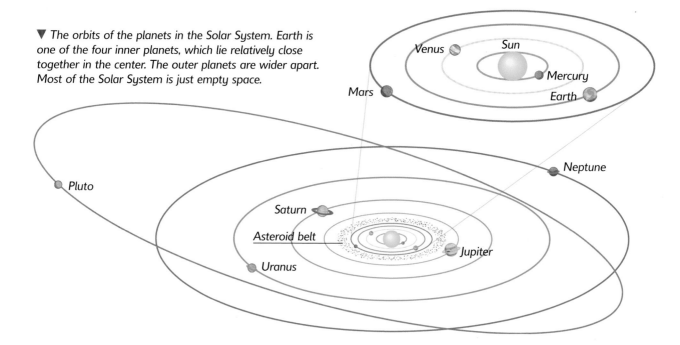

A.D.150). No one challenged this notion until 1543, when Polish astronomer Nicolaus Copernicus put forth the idea that Earth and the planets circle the Sun. Copernicus's solar system marks the dawn of modern astronomy. At that time, however, religious leaders refused to accept the idea that Earth was not the center of the Solar System—much less the center of the Universe—as Ptolemy suggested. Copernicus's theory became widely accepted a century later.

DWARFS AND GIANTS

Four rocky (terrestrial or Earthlike) planets—Mercury, Venus, Earth, and Mars—oribit fairly close together near the Sun. They differ greatly in size, mass, and consistency from the "gas giants"—Jupiter, Saturn, Uranus, and Neptune—the next four planets out from the Sun. Made up mainly of gas and liquid gas, each gas giant is many times the size of Earth. The outermost planet, Pluto, is a very tiny ice world very different from all the others. Its far-ranging, elliptical orbit sometimes brings it closer to the Sun than Neptune. These are the only two planets that appear to change positions with each other.

ESCAPING EARTH

Everything on Earth is held down by the powerful force of gravity, or Earth's "pull." In order to launch something into space, we use speed to overcome gravity. A satellite destined for Earth orbit needs a launching speed of about 17,500 miles per hour (28,000 kilometers per hour). Even then, satellites are still bound to Earth by gravity.

Launching a probe farther into the Solar System to a distant body is much more difficult. A probe needs to reach escape velocity—a launch speed of at least 25,000 miles per hour (40,000 kph)—to completely escape from Earth's gravity.

ORDER OF THE PLANETS

A useful method for recalling the planets' order from the Sun is by remembering this sentence: My Very Educated Mother Just Served Us Nine Pizzas. (Mercury, Venus, Earth, Mars, Jupiter, Saturn, Uranus, Neptune, Pluto.)

OTHER BODIES

Many other bodies belong to the Solar System. Most planets have natural satellites, or moons, circling them. While Earth has just one—the Moon—more than sixty moons orbit Jupiter.

A huge swarm of miniplanets called asteroids also circles the Sun mostly in an area known as the asteroid belt between Mars and Jupiter. Another huge swarm of bodies lurks at the very edge of the Solar System in the Kuiper Belt, outside the orbit of Neptune. They are visible only when they travel in toward the Sun, appearing to us as comets.

BRIEF ENCOUNTERS

Planets, moons, asteroids, comets, and the Sun all provide targets for probes. When a probe reaches its target, it may just fly by and continue on its way. Or its engine may fire to slow it down so that the planet's gravity captures it. It may then go into orbit around the planet or land on its surface.

When probes encounter their target body, they focus a variety of instruments on it. Cameras provide valuable images of the celestial object in visible light. Another class of instruments, known as radiometers, measures a variety of different wavelengths of the electromagnetic spectrum, including ultraviolet, infrared, and gamma rays. Analyzing a planet using these rays reveals much more information, such as details of cloud formations, temperature variations, and levels of harmful radiation.

Magnetometers detect the presence of magnetism in and around a planet or other celestial body. Magnetism influences an object's behavior: The Sun's magnetism, for example, causes cooler, darker areas known as sunspots to form on the solar surface.

Particle-detector instruments measure the amounts of electrically charged particles. Detectors reveal whether or not bands of particles—such as the Van Allen radiation belts that circle Earth—are found around other planets.

Most probes carry electronic equipment, including onboard computers and radio communications devices, that receives and responds to commands. Probes communicate with Earth over vast distances in order to send back instrument readings, images, and data.

TARGETING THE SUN

A series of Pioneer craft (numbered 5 to 9), launched between 1960 and 1968, were the first probes to study the Sun from space. *Helios 1* and *Helios 2* followed in 1974 and 1976, respectively, approaching

▲ Solar Max *is yet another satellite that targeted the Sun. This image shows the Sun's outer atmosphere.*

to within 27 million miles (43 million km) of the Sun. By this time, observations from the *Skylab* space station (1973–1974) had revolutionized solar study. *Skylab*'s astronauts conducted solar observations continuously for months at a time.

Ulysses, a European Space Agency (ESA) solar probe launched by the National Aeronautics and Space Administration ((NASA), broke new ground in 1990. It used the gravitational pull of Jupiter to swing it into an orbit that took it over the unexplored north and south poles of the Sun (*see* "gravity assist," page 11).

The spectacularly successful *SOHO* (*Solar and Heliospheric Observatory*) probe, a NASA/ESA spacecraft, began operating in 1995. Its solar orbit is 930,000 miles (1,500,000 km) from Earth.

SOHO OBSERVATIONS

SOHO observes all kinds of solar phenomena, such as sunspots, solar flares, prominences, the solar corona, and the solar wind.

• Sunspots are cooler, and therefore darker, regions on the Sun's surface.

• Flares are huge explosions in the lower part of the Sun's atmosphere. They can set off "sunquakes" on the surface, just like earthquakes on Earth.

• Prominences are great fountains of fiery gas that leap hundreds of thousands of miles above the Sun's surface.

• The corona ("crown") is the Sun's outer atmosphere. It is only visible from Earth during a total solar eclipse, when the Moon blocks out the Sun's brilliant surface.

• The solar wind is a stream of electrically charged particles, such as electrons and protons, that flows continuously out from the Sun's corona into the far reaches of space.

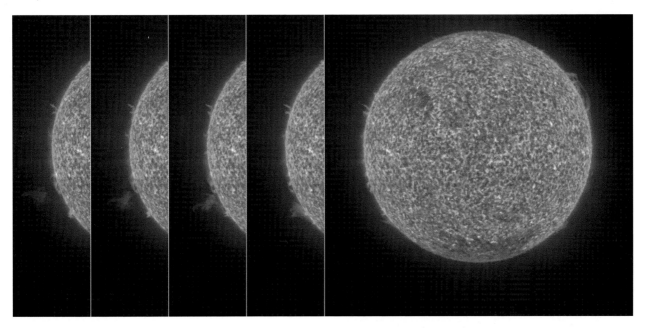

UNDER *SOHO*

SOHO examines the surface and atmosphere of the Sun continuously and in great detail. This continuous study is very important. The more information we gather about the Sun, the more we can hope to understand it and its effects on Earth. For example, the detailed study by *SOHO* of eruptions of particles from the Sun's corona, called coronal mass ejections (CMEs), helped us better understand the solar wind. CMEs increase the force of the solar wind, which often leads to magnetic storms on Earth. Such storms can knock out power stations, disrupt communications, and damage geostationary satellites.

▲ This **SOHO** *picture shows the Sun as it appears in ultraviolet light. The sequence of images shows the development of an "eruptive prominence," a blob of hot gas moving away from the solar surface at a speed of about 15,000 miles per hour (24,000 kph).*

▼ SOHO *observed the largest solar flare ever recorded in April 2001. Gas speeds away from the explosion in the huge bubble on the right.*

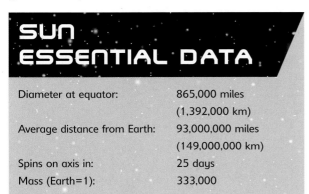

SUN ESSENTIAL DATA

Diameter at equator:	865,000 miles (1,392,000 km)
Average distance from Earth:	93,000,000 miles (149,000,000 km)
Spins on axis in:	25 days
Mass (Earth=1):	333,000

CHAPTER TWO

THE INNER PLANETS

Mercury and Venus, the two planets that orbit closer to the Sun than Earth, are quite different from each other. But they do have one thing in common— they are very hot. On both planets, temperatures can soar above 840° Fahrenheit (450° Celsius).

Mercury is a small world, approximately one-third the size of Earth. From Earth, we see it as a fairly bright "star," but it is often difficult to spot because it always stays close to the Sun in the sky. Like the other planets, Mercury gives out no light of its own; it shines only because it reflects sunlight. Even through powerful telescopes, we see only vague features on Mercury's surface. We discovered most of our knowledge about Mercury thanks to a single planetary probe called *Mariner 10*.

Launched in November 1973, *Mariner 10* flew on an indirect trajectory (flight path) to Mercury. It swung past Venus in February 1974, taking pictures of the cloud formations in Venus's atmosphere. Venus's gravity tugged at *Mariner 10*, increased its speed, and flung it into a new trajectory that allowed it to orbit Mercury three times. This marked the first "gravity-assist" maneuver ever attempted.

▶ Mariner 10 *returned the first image of Mercury in March 1974. The image shows the heavily cratered surface of the planet from a distance of about 3,340,000 miles (5,380,000 km).*

GRAVITY ASSIST

When employing the gravity-assist technique, a probe uses the gravitational energy of one planet to speed it on its way toward another planet. Flight controllers program the probe to fly close to the first planet. As the probe approaches the planet, the gravity of that planet pulls the probe toward itself, altering the probe's speed and direction. This combination of increased speed and direction change dramatically reduces journey times to a second planet. *Voyager 2* used this technique when it conducted its "grand tour" of the outer planets.

THE FLYBYS

Mariner 10 flew past Mercury first in March 1974, making a close approach of about 435 miles (700 km). It made a very distant pass in September, then a second close pass in March 1975, when it swooped to only about 200 miles (320 km) from the surface.

Mariner 10's twin TV cameras revealed a landscape almost completely covered with craters, like the heavily cratered regions of the Moon. But there are no great plains, or "seas," on Mercury as there are on the Moon. Mercury has some small plains regions and also areas where the surface is wrinkled or cut by steep cliffs and faults

(cracks). The 800-mile (1,300-km) -wide Caloris Basin, surrounded by concentric rings of mountain ranges, is probably Mercury's most noticeable surface feature.

▼ Mariner 10 *captured part of Mercury's Caloris Basin (left), ringed by a prominent mountain range.*

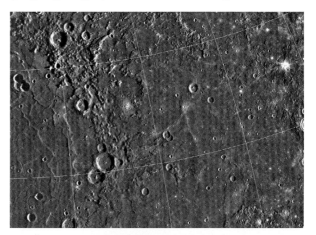

MERCURY ESSENTIAL DATA

Diameter at equator:	3,032 miles (4,880 km)
Average distance from Sun:	36,000,000 miles (58,000,000 km)
Time to orbit Sun:	88 days
Spins on axis in:	59 days
Mass (Earth=1):	0.06
Number of moons:	0

▲ Mariner 10 *shortly before being installed in its launch vehicle in September 1973. Its dish antenna measures nearly 4 feet (120 centimeters) across; each solar panel measures 8.8 feet (2.7 meters) long. Mariner 10 weighs about 1,100 pounds (500 kilograms).*

Mariner 10 also discovered Mercury's slight magnetic field. The planet's huge iron core that reaches three-quarters of the way to Mercury's surface produces its magnetism.

▲ *A valley more than 4 miles (6.5 km) wide runs into a crater on Mercury. The crater, which measures about 50 miles (80 km) across, has a very smooth floor.*

VISITS TO VENUS

Venus is the easiest planet to spot in the sky. It shines brightly as an "evening star" in the west after sunset during many months of the year. At other times, it's visible just before sunrise in the east as a "morning star." Venus shines so brightly—much brighter than any star—because it is the planet nearest Earth. At its closest, Venus lies only 26 million miles (42 million km) away from the Sun.

Venus is nearly the same size as Earth and, like Earth, it has an atmosphere filled with clouds. Early last century, some scientists thought that Venus was similar to Earth (see quote, below), but they were completely wrong. Venus's clouds are much thicker than Earth's and prevent us from seeing all the way down to its surface. Venus's atmosphere is also much denser than Earth's—its atmospheric pressure is ninety times that of Earth's.

> A very great part of the surface of Venus is no doubt covered with swamps, corresponding to those on the Earth in which the coal deposits were formed. . . . Only low forms of life are represented, mostly no doubt belonging to the vegetable kingdom.
> **Swedish scientist Svante Arrhenius, writing in 1918, describes what he thought Venus might be like.**

▲ *Mariner 10* captured this image of cloud patterns in Venus's atmosphere when it flew past the planet in February 1974.

Venus's atmosphere is hotter than any oven. The first sign of Venus's extraordinarily heat came when *Mariner 2* flew past the planet in August 1962. NASA launched *Mariner 2* toward Venus with these objectives: to pass near the planet, to communicate with the spacecraft from the planet, and to perform a meaningful planetary experiment. While these objectives seem modest now, at the time NASA had yet to conduct a successful mission to the Moon.

Mariner 2 performed flawlessly, flying past Venus at a distance of less than 21,700 miles (34,900 km). It found that the surface temperature was at least 800° F (425° C) and that the atmosphere was made up mainly of carbon dioxide.

After many failures, Soviet probes successfully targeted Venus in October 1967, when *Venera 4* parachuted into the atmosphere and returned data about conditions there. *Venera*s 5 and 6 were equally successful two years later. In 1970, *Venera 7* actually landed and sent back data from the surface, as did *Venera 8* in 1972. (*Venera 7* was the first man-made object to return data after landing on another planet.) All these probes confirmed the high-temperature, high-pressure conditions in the Venusian atmosphere.

In 1975, *Venera*s 9 and 10 broke new ground in space exploration because they consisted of two parts—one portion of the vehicle parachuted into the atmosphere and landed, while the other went into orbit around the planet. The Soviet landers returned the first images of Venus's surface, which revealed a rock-strewn landscape.

▶ *The* Venera 5 *space probe before launch in January 1969. In May, it dropped a 3.3-foot (1-m) -diameter capsule into Venus's atmosphere. Instruments in the capsule confirmed Venera 4's finding that the atmosphere contained mainly (up to 97 percent) carbon dioxide.*

VENUS ESSENTIAL DATA

Diameter at equator:	7,521 miles (12,104 km)
Average distance from Sun:	67,000,000 miles (108,000,000 km)
Time to orbit Sun:	224.7 days
Spins on axis in:	243 days
Mass (Earth=1):	0.8
Number of moons:	0

Although equipped with floodlights because scientists believed that the thick clouds covering Venus would make the surface too dark to photograph, the lights proved unnecessary. As a member of the Venera mission control team put it, the surface was "as bright as Moscow on a cloudy day in June."

SEEING THE SURFACE

NASA sent two craft to Venus in 1978 called *Pioneer Venus*. The first went into orbit, while the second plunged into the atmosphere after releasing three probes to parachute down.

The *Pioneer Venus* orbiter became the first craft to image the planet's surface on a large scale. It used radar to do this. Radar uses radio waves that can penetrate Venus's thick cloud cover. Radar works by transmitting pulses of radio signals and then picking up reflections from a surface. An analysis of the reflected signals yields a detailed description of those surface features.

The orbiter's radar showed a generally low-lying Venusian surface dotted with several highland regions —two large enough to be considered continents. Aphrodite Terra, which is about the size of Africa, lies near Venus's equator. Farther north is Ishtar Terra, which is about the size of Australia.

In the early 1980s, the Soviet Union sent several Venera probes to Venus. Some probes transmitted the first color images of the surface. Others scanned Venus's surface using radar.

Two Soviet Vega spacecraft launched in December 1984 also gathered interesting data on Venus. In June 1985, they dropped miniprobes that floated in Venus's atmosphere and recorded wind speeds as high as 150 miles per hour (240 kph). The main Vega probes, meanwhile, continued on their way toward a 1986 rendezvous with comet Halley.

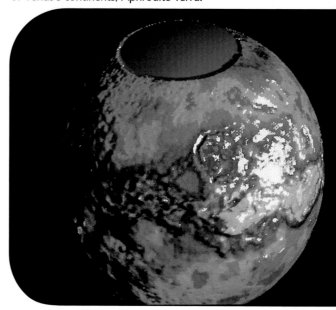

▼ *A model of Venus's surface produced from* Pioneer Venus's *radar scans. The most dominant feature is one of Venus's continents, Aphrodite Terra.*

VOLCANIC VISTAS

In 1990, NASA's *Magellan* probe went into orbit around Venus. Over the next four years, it mapped nearly 99 percent of the planet's surface. *Magellan* scanned the Venusian surface several times using high-resolution radar. The images captured incredible detail. They revealed a planet shaped almost entirely by volcanoes.

Venus has hundreds of volcanoes that erupt again and again, pouring out rivers of molten lava to create huge lava plains. Some of Venus's volcanic features are unique in the Solar System. These include circular lava "pancakes," crownlike structures called coronae—some of which span hundreds of miles (kilometers) across—and networks of surface faults (cracks) that look like spiders' webs. Scientists named the cracks arachnoids, from the Latin word for spider.

▶ *Venus's Gula Mons volcano, nearly 2 miles (3 km) high, sits on the horizon, about 812 miles (1,310 km) away from this viewpoint. The 30-mile (50-km) -wide impact crater Cunitz (right center), named after astronomer Marie Cunitz, lies about 133 miles (215 km) away from this viewpoint.*

MAGELLAN'S MISSION

The *Space Shuttle Atlantis* launched *Magellan* probe on May 5, 1989. Later, its attached rocket booster fired to speed it on its way to Venus. *Magellan* went into orbit around Venus on August 10, 1990; it began mapping the planet a month later.

Magellan followed an elliptical (oval) orbit around Venus. On its nearest approach to the planet, *Magellan* pointed its 12-foot (3.7-m) dish antenna toward the ground, scanned the surface with radar beams, and recorded the results. Then, as it swung away, it turned its antenna toward Earth and transmitted the data. On each orbit, *Magellan* scanned an area of the surface about 12 miles (20 km) wide and 10,000 miles (16,000 km) long. In four years, *Magellan* scanned more than 98 percent of Venus's surface before burning up in its atmosphere on October 11, 1994.

▶ Magellan *sits on top of its booster rocket in Atlantis's shuttle bay. Its solar panels are folded down.*

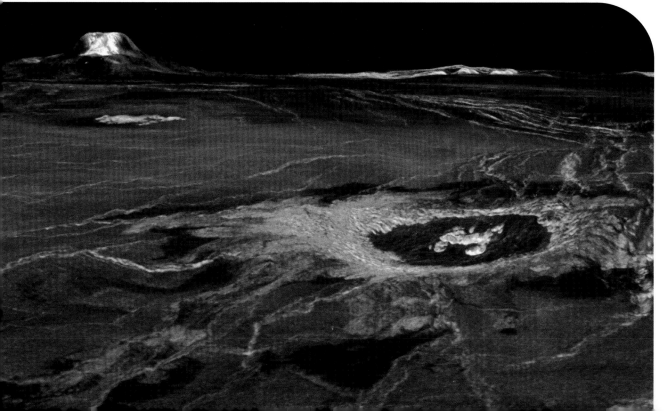

CHAPTER THREE

THE RED PLANET

Mars's fascinating fiery red color earned it the nickname the "Red Planet." As one of Earth's closer Solar System neighbors, it proved an obvious target for early probes.

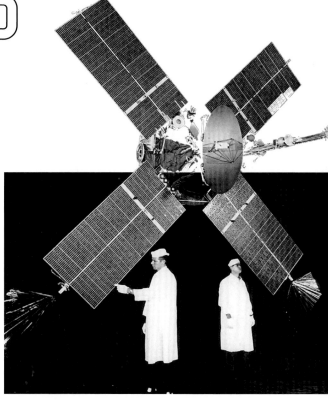

▲ The Mariner 4 *space probe transmitted the first close-up images of Mars. Technicians check out the craft before launch.*

Mars is one of the smallest planets—only about half the size of Earth in diameter. It is similar to Earth in some ways. Its "day" (the time it takes to spin around on its axis) is only a few minutes longer than ours. Mars also has seasons like Earth, and its north and south poles are covered with ice caps.

In the 1800s, people wondered whether Mars really might be like another Earth. In 1877, Italian astronomer Giovanni Schiaparelli reported seeing "canali" (channels) on Mars. Many people took this literally to mean canals, or artificial waterways. They began to think that intelligent beings on Mars dug canals to irrigate crops. Percival Lowell, an American astronomer and a strong believer in a Martian race, built an observatory in Flagstaff, Arizona, specifically to study Mars.

> " A mind of no mean order would seem to have presided over the system we see. Certainly what we see hints at the existence of beings who are in advance of, not behind, us in the journey of life. "
> **U.S. astronomer Percival Lowell, commenting on the "canals" on Mars.**

MARINERS TO MARS

The Soviet Union made at least five attempts to send probes to the Red Planet in 1960 and 1962, but all failed. The United States' first attempt, *Mariner 3*, in early November 1964 also failed.

An identical craft, *Mariner 4*, launched three weeks later and flew past Mars in July 1965. It transmitted only twenty-one images of the surface, the closest from a distance of less than 6,000 miles (9,600 km). They showed a barren, cratered landscape. *Mariner*s 6 and 7, which flew past the planet in July and August 1969, respectively, returned similar images. These images covered a larger part of the surface and showed no signs of canals. Data indicated that Mars's atmosphere consisted almost entirely of carbon dioxide.

Previous Mariner probes had flown past Mars, but *Mariner 9* actually orbited the planet in 1971, swooping down to within 870 miles (1,400 km) of the surface at its lowest point. *Mariner 9* spent nearly twelve months surveying the planet, photographing almost all of the surface.

Mariner 9's images showed a wide variety of surface features—huge, flat, desertlike regions, enormous basins, heavily cratered areas, and a number of spectacular volcanoes. One volcano, named Olympus Mons (Mount Olympus), is the largest known volcano in the Solar System. It rises from a base that measures 370 miles (600 km) across to a height of 15 miles (24 km).

MARS ESSENTIAL DATA

Diameter at equator:	4,222 miles (6,794 km)
Average distance from Sun:	142,000,000 miles (228,000,000 km)
Time to orbit Sun:	687 days
Spins on axis in:	24.6 hours
Mass (Earth=1):	0.11
Number of moons:	2

▼ *The volcano Olympus Mons, from* Mariner 9.

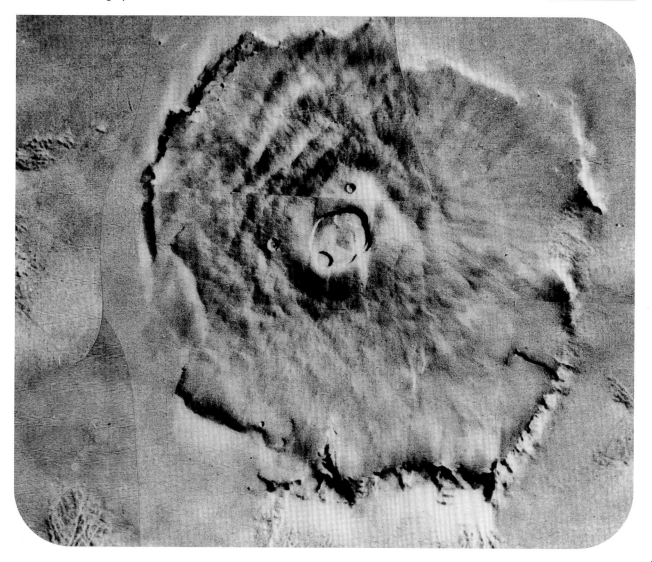

Mariner 9 also discovered a huge surface-fault system, named Valles Marineris (Mariner Valley), running along Mars's equator. Nicknamed Mars's Grand Canyon, it is much bigger than Arizona's—2,800 miles (4,500 km) long and 5 miles (8 km) deep in places. By contrast, Arizona's famous Grand Canyon runs for about 200 miles (320 km) along the Colorado River and is at most only a little more than 1 mile (1.6 km) deep.

Unlike Earth's Grand Canyon, Valles Marineris was created not by a river flowing through it, but when Mars's crust cracked. *Mariner* 9 imaged many other channel-like martian features that look as if flowing water formed them. Perhaps the Red Planet once had a milder, wetter climate than it does now. Could some form of life have also developed?

THE VIKING INVASION

While *Mariner* 9 reported back from Mars, NASA finalized its plans for the next set of Red Planet probes, the identical spacecraft, *Viking 1* and *2*. Both were programmed to take high-resolution images from orbit as well as close-up images as the

▼ The Viking I *probe being checked in a laboratory before its long journey to Mars in 1976.*

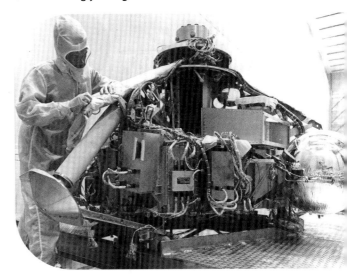

landers dropped down to the martian surface. The landers sent information to their orbiters, which in turn transmitted it back to Earth.

The *Viking 1* and *2* probes launched in August and September 1975, respectively, entered martian orbit in June and August 1976. After searching the surface for a suitable landing site, *Viking 1* dropped

▼ Viking 1 *sent back this image of the surface at Chryse Planitia. Small rocks litter the martian surface.*

its lander down safely in a region called Chryse Planitia ("The Plains of Gold") in July. The lander used parachutes, then fired retrorockets that slowed it down enough to make a soft landing. *Viking 2* made landfall 4,000 miles (6,500 km) away, in a region known as Utopia Planitia, in September 1976.

THROUGH VIKINGS' EYES

Although the two probes landed far apart, they revealed that the surface at both locations looked remarkably similar. Images showed reddish rocks and boulders strewn about the reddish soil. Fine dust blown up from the frequent martian dust storms gave the sky a yellowish-brown, nearly pink tinge.

Meteorological instruments on the landers registered wind speeds up to about 30 miles per hour (50 kph). They also recorded weather patterns, seasonal changes, and temperatures ranging from daytime highs up to 80° F (25° C) to nighttime lows that dipped to –190° F (–125° C).

A digging arm on each Viking craft fed martian soil samples into its biological laboratory. The probes tested samples for signs of life but found none. Overall, both Viking missions were outstandingly

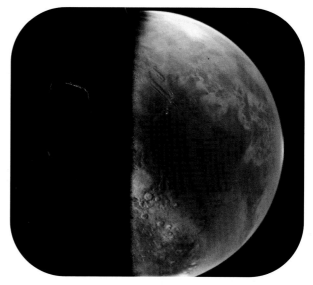

▲ Viking 1 *snapped this picture of Mars the day before it went into orbit around the planet on June 19, 1976.*

It's just a beautiful collection of boulders—a geologist's dream! This is just incredible good luck!
Tim Mutch, Viking mission geologist, as the first images came in from the *Viking 1* lander.
Fine and sunny. Very cold. Winds light and variable. Further outlook similar.
Garry Hunt, Viking mission scientist, giving a "weather forecast" for the Chryse region where *Viking 1* landed.

▼ *Utopia Planitia, from* Viking 2. *The landscape looks remarkably similar to that of Chryse Planitia.*

successful. The *Viking 1* orbiter and lander remained active until August 1980 and November 1982, repectively; *Viking 2* until July 1978 and April 1980.

LOOKING FOR LIFE

Viking landers carried out a series of experiments in their search for signs of martian life. (Any living organism on Earth absorbs radioactive carbon during its lifetime.) The landers subjected the soil samples—taken from the sunlit martian surface—to extreme temperatures and measured any gases released by the process.

The experiments were based on the theory that fierce heating converts (changes) any organic material (material from living things) into carbon dioxide gas. The presence of radioactive carbon in the gas would suggest the possible presence of living organisms in the sample. Neither lander revealed any trace of organic compounds in soil tests at its site.

Since then, NASA scientists have devised a new experiment that mimics martian conditions and indicates that the absence of radioactive carbon does not necessarily rule out the absence of life.

▼ *A panoramic view of the landscape around Pathfinder, showing parts of the probe in the foreground.*

MORE VISITS TO MARS

In the 1990s and early years of the twenty-first century, many probes set off for Mars, but not all made it. NASA's *Mars Observer* (launched 1992) failed before it entered orbit around Mars. The next two missions were highly successful, however.

Launched in 1996, the *Mars Global Surveyor* was still operating eight years later. It mapped Mars in fine detail from orbit, providing a wealth of new geological data on the Red Planet. *Pathfinder* landed on July 4, 1997, carrying a small rover called *Sojourner* that analyzed nearby rocks.

▲ *The* Pathfinder *probe and the rover* Sojourner *(left) pictured on the Martian surface in an artist's montage of an actual* Pathfinder *photograph.*

After losing two probes in 1999 (*Mars Climate Orbiter* and *Mars Polar Lander*), NASA achieved success again when *Mars Odyssey* went into martian orbit in 2001. Its instruments analyzed the surface and found substantial amounts of water ice over vast regions of the planet.

Three probes launched in the summer of 2003 began operations about six months later. The ESA's *Mars Express Orbiter* slipped into martian orbit in December 2003. Earlier, it released a lander, *Beagle 2*, designed to examine the rocks and soil for signs of life. Unfortunately, all communications with the *Beagle 2* were lost.

NASA's *Mars Express Orbiter* worked perfectly, however, and soon began sending back the most detailed images ever of the martian surface. It also detected the presence of water in the south polar ice cap and in the atmosphere.

ROVING AROUND

Two identical NASA probes touched down on Mars in January 2004. *Spirit* landed first (on January 4) in a large crater named Gusev; *Opportunity* landed three weeks later on the opposite side of the planet in a region known as Meridiana Planitia, just east of Valles Marineris. *Spirit* and *Opportunity* were both rovers—vehicles designed to move around the surface. Each about the size of a golf cart, the rovers acted as robot geologists. A robotic arm on *Spirit* and *Opportunity* included a drilling tool as well as spectroscopes for analyzing rocks.

Both rovers had six wheels that could be steered independently. Each rover carried "engineering hazard avoidance" cameras that helped it "see" its way around and select a path that avoided any obstacles. Two navigation cameras helped guide it, and two science panoramic cameras imaged the surface. Finally, a science microscope imager took pictures of mineral samples.

▶ *Close-up of a rock, nicknamed Humphrey, targeted by* Spirit *in February 2004.* Spirit's *drill cut the hole in the center of Humphrey.*

The Mars rovers sent back a wealth of interesting images and data. For example, *Opportunity* photographed rocks that showed distinct layering, suggesting that they formed from layers of sediment deposited in ancient salty seas.

▼ Spirit *took this panoramic view of the martian surface in January 2004. It shows a range of rolling hills on the distant horizon.*

CHAPTER FOUR

LOOKING AT GIANTS

Beyond Mars and the asteroid belt lie Jupiter and Saturn, two enormous planets targeted by probes since the 1970s. They are truly the giants among the planets: Jupiter alone has more than twice the mass of all the other planets put together.

Jupiter is truly gigantic, more than eleven times bigger across than Earth. In telescopes, we see clouds in the Jovian atmosphere stretched out into parallel bands by the planet's rapid rotation. Throughout its atmosphere, all kinds of streaks, swirls, and ovals indicate stormy weather on the planet. The biggest storm feature, an oval called the Great Red Spot, is as big as about three of Earth's widths across.

Cloud bands also cross Saturn's atmosphere, but they are much less prominent than Jupiter's. Saturn's main feature is the system of shining rings that circle the equator, making it the most beautiful of the planets through a telescope.

THE GRAND TOUR

In 1969, NASA scientists began working on a project they called the Grand Tour. This was a multiplanet mission designed to take advantage of an upcoming alignment (lining up) of the outer planets that would not happen again for more than 170 years.

The plan was brilliant—because of the alignment, a spacecraft launched to Jupiter could use Jupiter's gravity to boost it to Saturn; Saturn's gravity to boost it to Uranus; and Uranus's gravity to boost it to Neptune. NASA named the project Voyager. It called for the launch of two identical spacecraft: They would program *Voyager 1* to visit only Jupiter and Saturn. *Voyager 2* would attempt the Grand Tour of all four giant outer planets.

JUPITER ESSENTIAL DATA

Diameter at equator:	88,900 miles (143,000 km)
Average distance from Sun:	483,000,000 miles (778,000,000 km)
Time to orbit Sun:	11.9 years
Spins on axis in:	9.9 hours
Mass (Earth=1):	318
Number of moons:	61

SATURN ESSENTIAL DATA

Diameter at equator:	74,900 miles (120,500 km)
Average distance from Sun:	891,000,000 miles (1,434,000,000 km)
Time to orbit Sun:	29.5 years
Spins on axis in:	10.7 hours
Mass (Earth=1):	95
Number of moons:	30

▲ Voyager *encounters Saturn in an imaginative piece of NASA artwork. The illustration shows the probe's journey through the Solar System from Earth via Jupiter.*

BLAZING THE TRAIL

In the early 1970s, two Pioneer craft blazed a trail for the Voyager probes to come. *Pioneer 10* began its journey to Jupiter in 1972; one year later, *Pioneer 11* also left for Jupiter and possibly on to Saturn.

Unlike satellites that use solar cells for energy, probes launched toward the outer reaches of the Solar System need nuclear "batteries," called radioisotope thermoelectric generators (RTGs), for energy sources. Sunlight in the gas giant area of the Solar System is simply too weak to power a spacecraft.

PIONEERING FLIGHTS

Pioneer 10 was boosted away from Earth in March 1972 at more than 32,000 miles per hour (51,500 kph), the highest speed yet reached by a man-made object. The hearty probe faced a journey of more than 600 million miles (1 billion km) through the uncharted regions of space. By July of that year, *Pioneer 10* began its eight-month trek through the asteroid belt—considered the most dangerous part

of the entire mission. A collision with even a tiny asteroid would be fatal for the craft. But, remarkably, *Pioneer 10* survived undamaged. In December 1973, it flew past Jupiter at a distance of about 81,000 miles (130,000 km).

▲ *A NASA illustration of* Pioneer 10 *flying over Jupiter's Great Red Spot. Two nuclear units that power the probe stick out from behind* Pioneer 10's *dish antennae.*

PIONEER 10

On March 2, 1972, *Pioneer 10* set out from Earth to explore regions of space "where nothing built by humanity had ever gone before," said Colleen Hartman, director of NASA's Solar System Exploration Division. Originally designed for a twenty-one-month mission to explore Jupiter, *Pioneer 10* continually transmitted space data for more than thirty years. It sent its last meaningful data on April 27, 2002. NASA received a final feeble signal from it on January 22, 2003. By then, *Pioneer 10* was 7.6 billion miles (12.2 billion km) from Earth. It continues to coast silently through space toward Aldebaran, the bright, reddish star that marks the eye of the bull in the constellation we call Taurus.

Pioneer 10 sent back the best pictures of Jupiter yet, showing details of the cloud circulating around and within the Great Red Spot. Instrument data showed that the planet is almost all liquid, with no solid surface. Hydrogen and helium are the main gases in the atmosphere. Just like Earth, Jupiter has magnetism, but its magnetism is 20,000 times greater. And like Earth, doughnut-shaped regions of radiation belts also ring Jupiter, but they, too, are much more intense than Earth's Van Allen radiation belts. In fact, the radiation knocked out some of *Pioneer 10*'s instruments. Afterwards, *Pioneer 10* began heading out of the Solar System.

Pioneer 11 stayed in orbit around Jupiter until December 1974. Then, it used a gravity-assist manueuver to go around Jupiter one last time, setting off on a journey of almost five years to Saturn.

THE PIONEER PLAQUE

It is possible that, in tens of thousands of years time, intelligent beings from another planet around another star may find the *Pioneer 10* and *11* probes. They each carry a plaque with graphics that explain to alien beings where they originated and who sent them. Whether or not the alien beings could decipher the plaques is another matter. U.S. astronomers Frank Drake and Carl Sagan devised the Pioneer plaque; Sagan's wife, Ann Druyan, drew it.

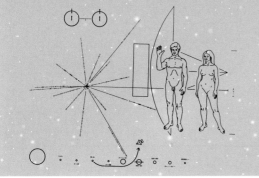

VOYAGERS TO JUPITER

Encouraged by the Pioneer flights, NASA finalized the details for the Voyager missions. The spacecraft had better science instruments and imaging systems. They too carried a "message to aliens" in the form of a record disk called "Sounds of Earth." The disk contained the sights and sounds of the natural and man-made world and messages from world leaders (*see* page 31).

▲ *A close-up Voyager picture of Jupiter's Great Red Spot, an enormous atmospheric storm that has been blowing for centuries.*

Voyager 2 was launched on August 20, 1977, about sixteen days before *Voyager 1*. Both survived passage through the asteroid belt. *Voyager 1* reached Jupiter first, flying past in March 1979; *Voyager 2* followed four months later. Both left Jupiter and headed for their next destination—Saturn.

The Voyagers returned thousands of fantastic images of Jupiter and discovered a faint ring around the planet. They also discovered three new tiny moons and captured revealing close-up images of Jupiter's four large Galilean moons. Named after Galileo, the Italian astronomer and physicist who first

◀ Voyager 1 snapped this picture of Jupiter in February 1979. At top left is the Great Red Spot; near the bottom is the moon Io.

saw them, these moons all proved very different from one another. Callisto is covered in craters; Europa is incredibly smooth; Ganymede has dark and light regions, peppered with fresh white craters. But Io caused the greatest surprise. It is vividly colored, red, orange, and yellow and has active volcanoes. The Voyagers saw several erupting volcanoes that shot material high above the surface. Rather than molten lava, the ejected material is sulfur.

"Io looks better than a lot of pizzas I've seen.
Larry Soderblom, Voyager imaging team, introducing images of Jupiter's garishly colored moon Io, afterward nicknamed the "pizza moon.""

▼ *Voyager 1 captured this image of a volcano erupting on Io's skyline, blasting gas and particles high above the surface.*

ON TO SATURN

In August 1979, as *Voyager 2* began its two-year journey to Saturn, *Pioneer 11* was approaching the ringed planet. The latter probe quickly discovered a new ring (labeled F) just outside the outer A ring visible from Earth and found evidence of a G ring even farther out.

Because of their different trajectories, *Voyager 1* arrived at Saturn in August 1980, ten months before *Voyager 2*. Together, the probes made many discoveries, particularly about the rings.

Scientists determined that the rings consist of thousands of separate ringlets, made up of millions of icy pieces, up to several feet across, whizzing around the planet at high speed.

The Voyagers spotted the new rings (F and G) that *Pioneer 11* had identified and found another broad, faint ring (E) beyond the G ring. The spacecraft also discovered three tiny moons. Two

▼ A montage of images taken by Voyager 1 *during its encounter with Saturn. In the foreground is the moon Dione, with Saturn behind. Top left are the moons Enceladus and Rhea, and at the bottom right, Tethys and Mimas. Titan lies at top right.*

orbited on either side of the F ring. These became known as the "shepherd moons" because they appeared to keep the ring particles in place.

Saturn's largest moon, Titan, also provided a unique surprise: It had an atmosphere—and one that was more than one-and-a-half times denser than Earth's.

▲ A Voyager 2 *image of Saturn's rings. Each ring consists of thousands of separate ringlets.*

After their encounters with Saturn, *Voyager 1* left to head out of the Solar System, but *Voyager 2* still had two calls to make, on Uranus and Neptune.

GALILEO TO JUPITER

In 1979, NASA considered plans for a longer-term investigation of the giant planet before the Voyagers even reached Jupiter. They named the project *Galileo*, after the astronomer who pioneered the use of the telescope and discovered Jupiter's four big moons.

The *Galileo* probe was finally launched in October 1989 from the Space Shuttle *Atlantis*. It faced a six-year journey that boosted its speed using gravity-assist maneuvers at Venus (once) and Earth (twice). This journey took *Galileo* twice through the asteroid belt, where the probe seized the opportunity to photograph asteroids Gaspra and Ida for the first time (*see* page 34 for an image of Gaspra).

Galileo went into orbit around Jupiter in 1995, after dropping a small probe into the atmosphere. Over the next eight years, it sent back images and data on Jupiter and its four major moons, Callisto, Gannymede, Io, and Europa—the latter two of which proved very interesting. Galileo also confirmed the existence of a large ocean—that some scientists believed could contain primitive life-forms—under Europa's icy surface.

WHAT'S IN A NAME?

The *Cassini-Huygens* probe to Saturn is named after two astronomers who made significant discoveries about the planet. Italian astronomer Giovanni Domenico Cassini discovered four of Saturn's satellites and the main divisions (A, B, and C) in its rings. Dutch astronomer Christiaan Huygens discovered Saturn's largest moon Titan, target of the Huygens lander. Other probes or satellites named after notable astronomers or scientists include the following spacecraft:

Chandra X-ray Observatory (for Subrahmanyan Chandrasekhar)

Compton Gamma Ray Observatory (for Arthur Holly Compton)

Galileo (for Galileo Galilei)

Hubble Space Telescope (for Edwin Hubble)

Magellan (for Ferdinand Magellan)

NEAR-Shoemaker (for Eugene Shoemaker)

Spitzer Space Telescope (for Lyman Spitzer)

CASSINI TO SATURN

Cassini-Huygens is a NASA/European Space Agency probe designed to carry out a four-year, in-depth investigation of Saturn, its rings, and its moons. Launched in October 1997, *Cassini-Huygens* also used a series of gravity-assist maneuvers (at Venus, Earth, and Jupiter) to reach its target. It is scheduled to enter orbit around Saturn in July 2004. Later, it will launch a miniprobe to land on Titan and report back from its surface.

▲ The Huygens *probe drops down toward Titan in this artist's impression of the* Cassini-Huygens *mission to Saturn and Titan. The* Cassini *spacecraft in the background is shown in orbit around Saturn.*

CHAPTER FIVE

DISCOVERING NEW WORLDS

The three planets beyond Saturn—Uranus, Neptune, and Pluto—are too far away to be seen with the naked eye. Of these, only Pluto has not been visited yet by space probes. Uranus and Neptune were the final planetary targets of the amazingly successful *Voyager 2*.

Early astronomers thought that there were only six planets, with Saturn the most distant. In 1781, English astronomer William Herschel discovered a seventh planet, which was named Uranus. It proved to be twice as far away from the Sun as Saturn. At a stroke, the size of the known Solar System had doubled.

German astronomer Johann Galle discovered an eighth planet—Neptune—on September 23, 1846, and U.S. astronomer Clyde Tombaugh discovered a ninth—Pluto—on February 18, 1930.

A CURIOUS NEBULOUS STAR

On March 13, 1781, German-born musician-turned-astronomer William Herschel was looking through a telescope at the stars in the constellation Gemini at his home in Bath, England. He saw an object that he thought was a "curious nebulous star or perhaps a comet." It was neither. Herschel had spied a new planet—the first planet discovered since ancient times. It was named Uranus.

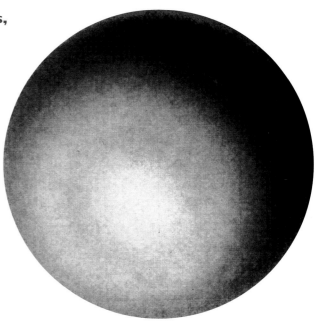

▲ Uranus is perhaps the least interesting planet to view. It appears bluish-green all over, with no obvious features. Computer-enhanced Voyager 2 images reveals some details, such as hazy regions around the planet's poles.

VOYAGER'S URANUS

The planet Uranus is about four times bigger across than Earth. One strange thing about Uranus is that it spins on its side compared with all the other planets. In telescopes, it looks like a bluish-green star. A set of faint rings was discovered around it in 1977. At that time, astronomers also knew it had five moons.

Little was known about what Uranus was really like until *Voyager 2* flew past it. The probe used Saturn's gravity in August 1981 to increase its speed and direct it away from the sixth planet into a trajectory toward Uranus. *Voyager 2* made a close approach to within about 50,000 miles (80,000 km) of Uranus in January 1986.

Voyager's images showed that Uranus looks much the same all over, a hazy bluish-green. Methane gas in the atmosphere, which is made up mainly of hydrogen and helium, produces the color.

Looking at Uranus's ring system, *Voyager 2* spotted a total of eleven rings. The outermost ring, the Epsilon, is the brightest. All the rings appear to be composed of particles about 3.3 feet (1 m) across. *Voyager 2* discovered a swarm of new moons around Uranus, all much nearer the planet than the known moons and much smaller. A pair of moons orbit on either side of the Epsilon ring and seem to act as shepherd moons to keep the ring particles in

URANUS ESSENTIAL DATA

Diameter at equator:	31,750 miles (51,100 km)
Average distance from Sun:	1,784,000,000 miles (2,871,000,000 km)
Time to orbit Sun:	84 years
Spins on axis in:	17.2 hours
Mass (Earth=1):	14.5
Number of moons:	27

place. Voyager 2 also imaged Uranus's five original moons clearly for the first time. They all proved to be very different from one another. The smallest of them, Miranda, has an amazing surface, made up of a patchwork of totally different landscapes.

▼ *Uranus's moon Miranda has an extraordinary surface. Some astronomers have suggested that it was produced when the moon was shattered into pieces in a collision with another body, and then reformed when the pieces came together.*

▲ *Uranus's rings show up clearly in this long-exposure* Voyager 2 *picture. The short, almost vertical streaks in the picture are star trails.*

VOYAGER'S NEPTUNE

After its success at Uranus, *Voyager 2* looped around the planet and headed toward its last planetary target, Neptune. At the time, little was known about this planet. It is a near twin of Uranus in size, with just two moons.

Voyager 2 made its closest approach to Neptune in August 1989. It skimmed just 3,050 miles (4,900 km) above the planet's cloud tops. This was a truly remarkable feat of navigation by the *Voyager 2* team over a period of twelve years and a distance of some 4.4 billion miles (7 billion km).

Images of Neptune showed a planet a deeper blue color and one with much more atmospheric activity than Uranus. Unlike Uranus's bland atmosphere, Neptune's contained several cloudy, dark-oval, stormy regions. Astronomers named the largest of these areas the Great Dark Spot (GDS), after Jupiter's Great Red Spot. *Hubble* revealed that Neptune's GDS has since disappeared, but a new Dark Spot formed elsewhere.

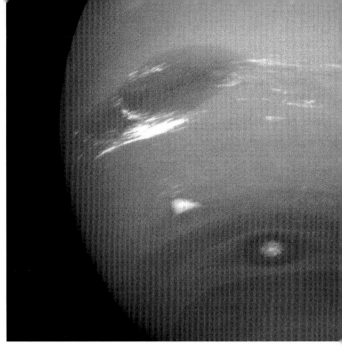

▲ *Neptune from* Voyager 2. *The most prominent feature is the Great Dark Spot (center), a violent storm region.*

As at the other planets it visited, *Voyager 2* also discovered new moons of Neptune. It found six small ones much closer to the planet than the two known moons. It also spotted a set of faint rings—two narrow and relatively bright and two broad and faint. This meant that all of the Gas Giants had rings.

FAREWELL

As a finale, *Voyager 2* sped on to view Neptune's biggest moon, Triton. It sent back stunning images

NEPTUNE ESSENTIAL DATA

Diameter at equator:	30,760 miles (49,500 km)
Average distance from Sun:	2,795,000,000 miles (4,498,000,000 km)
Time to orbit Sun:	164.8 years
Spins on axis in:	16.1 hours
Mass (Earth=1):	17.2
Number of moons:	13

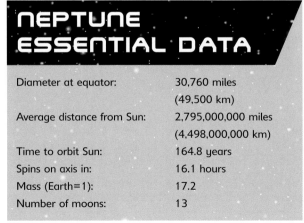

◀ *Bands of methane clouds show up in Neptune's atmosphere.*

showing a deep-frozen world at a temperature of −390° F (−235° C), the lowest temperature of any body in the Solar System. Yet volcanoes erupted on this frozen world. The extreme cold meant that these volcanoes did not pour out red-hot molten lava like those on Earth do, but are instead strange ice volcanoes that spew either very cold liquid or gaseous nitrogen, which then freezes.

> This is a present from a small, distant world, a token of our sounds, our science, our images, our music, our thoughts, and our feelings. We are attempting to survive our time so we may live into yours. We hope someday, having solved the problems we face, to join a community of galactic civilizations. This record represents our hopes and our determination, and our goodwill in a vast and awesome universe.
>
> **Message from U.S. president Jimmy Carter on the "Sounds of Earth" record disk carried by the Voyager probes.**

Voyager 2's discoveries at Triton marked a fitting end to the most remarkable feat of planetary exploration ever. The probe is now winging its way toward the edge of the Solar System. At some point around the year 2020, *Voyager 2* will cross a region known as the heliopause, which marks the outer edge of the Solar System, and begin it journey into interstellar space—the space between the stars.

PLUTO ESSENTIAL DATA

Diameter at equator:	1,485 miles (2,390 km)
Average distance from Sun:	3,666,000,000 miles (5,900,000,000 km)
Time to orbit Sun:	247.7 years
Spins on axis in:	6.4 days
Mass (Earth=1):	0.002
Number of moons:	1 (Charon)

▼ Neptune's biggest moon, Triton, measures 840 miles (1,350 km) across. Its surface seems to consist mainly of nitrogen ice, with some methane ice.

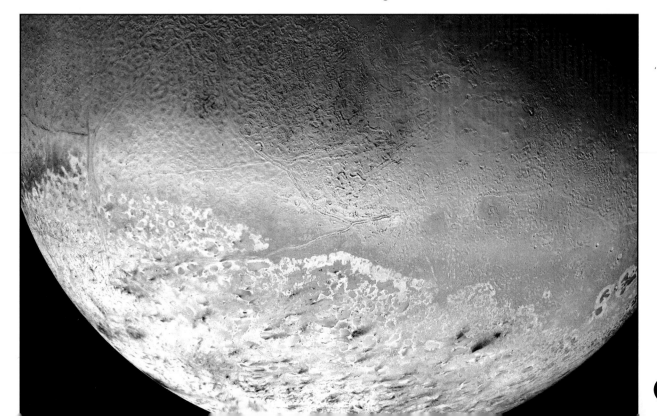

CHAPTER SIX

COMETS AND ASTEROIDS

Probes not only target the large members of the Solar System but also the smaller ones. Comets are tiny icy lumps that blaze into life when they near the Sun. They produce long tails of dust and gas that can extend for millions of miles.

NASA first sent a probe to a comet as an afterthought. Four years after it launched a small probe called *ISEE-3* (*International Sun-Earth Explorer 3*) in August 1978 to study the solar wind, mission controllers began painstakingly maneuvering the craft so that it could meet comet Giacobini-Zinner. Now renamed *ICE* (*International Comet Explorer*), the probe flew through the tail of the comet in September 1985. It detected ions (charged atoms) of water and carbon monoxide in the tail region.

FLOTILLA TO HALLEY

As *ICE* reported back from one comet, a flotilla of five probes headed for another—Halley's comet. They were planning to encounter the comet in March 1986 on one of its regular appearances in Earth's skies (it returns about every seventy-six years).

The flotilla included *Giotto* (from the European Space Agency), *Sakigake* and *Suisei* (from Japan), and *Vega 1* and *2* (from the Soviet Union). The two Japanese probes made distant flybys of the comet. But *Vega 1* and *2* flew into the coma,

◄ The *Giotto probe under construction. About 9 feet (2.8 m) high, it measures just over 6 feet (1.8 m) in diameter.*

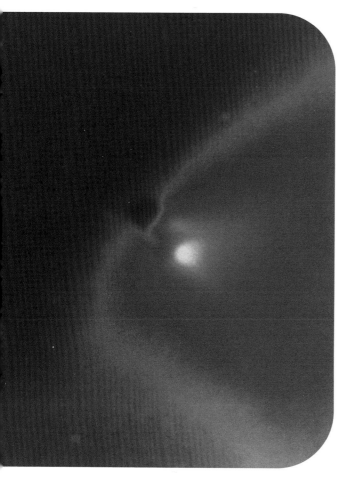

▲ Close-up image of Halley's comet returned by Giotto, shows the dark nucleus and bright jets of gas and dust coming from it.

or head, of the comet at a distance of about 5,000 miles (8,000 km) from the comet's solid nucleus.

Giotto plunged into the coma and made the closest encounter of all, passing only 375 miles (605 km) away from the nucleus. Despite being battered by dust particles, it returned amazing pictures showing brilliant jets of gas and dust shooting out of different parts of the nucleus. The nucleus itself was very dark in color and measured about 10 miles (16 km) long. Despite being damaged, Giotto managed to visit another comet, Grigg-Skjellerup, in 1992.

BORRELLY AND WILD

In 2001, a probe finally returned a better image of a comet nucleus. That probe was *Deep Space-1* (*DS-1*); the comet, Borrelly. NASA launched *DS-1* in 1998 to test new technologies, in particular ion propulsion. An ion motor produces power by giving off a stream of ions that propel (push) it forward. It does not produce much of a thrust, but the thrust builds on itself for long periods. Before visiting Borrelly, *DS-1* rendezvoused with asteroid Braille in July 1999.

> It's mind-boggling and stupendous. These pictures have told us that comet nuclei are far more complex than we ever imagined. They have rugged terrain, smooth rolling plains, deep fractures, and very, very dark material.
> **Larry Soderblom, *Deep Space 1* imaging team, after the probe's flyby of comet Borrelly in 2001.**

▼ The nucleus of comet Wild-2, photographed by Stardust. It measures about 3 miles (5 km) across.

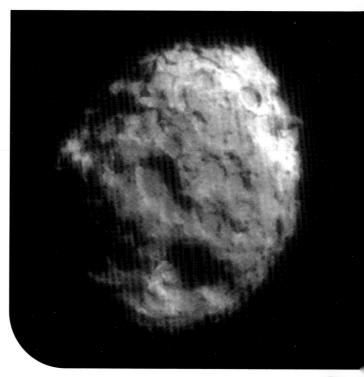

In February 1999, another exciting comet mission, named *Stardust,* got underway. *Stardust*'s objectives included an encounter early in 2004 with comet Wild-2 (pronounced "Vilt-Two"). It would also capture images, collect some of the dust around the comet, and return the dust to Earth in 2006.

Stardust flew closest to the comet on January 4, 2004, picking up dust streaming from the comet with its paddlelike collector. The photographs it took of the comet's nucleus showed unexpectedly sharp surface features. Usually, repeated heating of a comet's surface by the Sun softens features. The probe is due to arrive back to Earth in January 2006, when a capsule containing the dust is scheduled to reenter the atmosphere and be recovered and tested.

> "We were amazed by the feature-rich surface of the comet. It is highly complex. There are barn-sized boulders, 100-meter high cliffs, and some weird terrain unlike anything we've ever seen before. There are also some circular features that look like impact craters as large as one kilometer across."
>
> **Stardust principal investigator, Donald Brownlee, after the probe's encounter with comet Wild-2.**

The European Space Agency's probe *Rosetta* began an even more ambitious comet mission on March 2, 2004. It aims to orbit comet Churyumov-Gerasimenko in 2014 and drop a lander to touch down on the surface of the nucleus.

ASTEROID ENCOUNTERS

The rocky bodies known as asteroids are found mainly between the orbits of Mars and Jupiter. Astronomers believe that asteroids are leftover lumps from the beginning of the Solar System—lumps unable to clump together to form another planet.

CATCHING COMET DUST

Stardust used a material called aerogel to capture the minute specks of dust given off by comet Wild-2. Aerogel slows down and catches particles—which may travel at six times the speed of a rifle bullet—without altering them physically. A silicon-based substance, aerogel is 1,000 times lighter (less dense) than glass, a more familiar silicon-based material. Aerogel's highly porous structure is 99.8 percent air. When a particle enters aerogel, which is almost transparent, it leaves behind a visible track. Some people say aerogel resembles frozen smoke.

The biggest asteroid (Ceres) is only about 580 miles (930 km) across; most are much smaller.

Astronomers have spotted thousands of asteroids through telescopes, but they did not see one close up until 1991, when the *Galileo* probe flew past Gaspra on its way to Jupiter. Gaspra is an irregular lump of rock about 12 miles (20 km) long. Its surface is peppered with craters from collisions with smaller rocks. In general, most asteroids seem to consist mainly of rock. But others are made up of metal or mixtures of rock and metal.

▲ Gaspra was the first asteroid photographed from close quarters, by Galileo in 1991.

Two years later, *Galileo* imaged another asteroid, Ida. Although Ida is only about 34 miles (55 km) long, it has a moon named Dactyl. The moon is only about 1 mile (1.6 km) across.

MATHILDE AND EROS

Many asteroids wander away from the main asteroid belt, both out toward Saturn and in toward the inner planets. Some orbit fairly close to Earth. Eros, for example, comes within 14 million miles (22 million km)—much closer than the planets Venus and Mars.

When the probe *NEAR* (*Near Earth Asteroid Rendezvous*)-Shoemaker set off in February 1996, Eros was its target. After viewing asteroid Mathilde from close quarters in 1997, *NEAR* slipped into orbit around Eros on February 14, 2000. Two days short of a year later, *NEAR-Shoemaker* took high-resolution images as it descended to land on the surface of Eros. It was a remarkable feat considering that the probe was not originally designed for landing on anything.

▼ *Asteroid Eros from* NEAR-Shoemaker. *It measures about 21 miles (33 km) long and 8 miles (13 km) across.*

▼ *A NASA artist's impression of* NEAR-Shoemaker *in orbit around Eros. It spent a year orbiting the asteroid.*

CHAPTER SEVEN

PROBING DEEP SPACE

Our Solar System makes up a tiny part of an enormous Universe filled with stars, galaxies, and vast expanses of empty space. We study the visible light and other radiation emitted by these celestial bodies to learn about our great Universe.

The Earth we live on is a tiny speck of matter in the Universe. With the other planets, it circles the Sun, our local star. The Sun is only one of a huge family of about 200 billion stars. They group together to form a galaxy, a gigantic star island in space. We call our galaxy the Milky Way. Tens of billions of galaxies are scattered throughout space, and they too gather together into clusters. All these clusters together comprise our Universe.

▼ *The dome of the famous Hale Telescope in California, the first giant telescope, which saw "first light" in 1949.*

I have observed the nature and material of the Milky Way. . . . The Galaxy is in fact nothing but congeries (collections) of innumerable stars grouped together in clusters. Upon whatever part of it the telescope is directed, a vast cloud of stars is immediately presented to view, many of them rather large and quite bright, while the number of smaller ones is quite beyond calculation.
Italian astronomer Galileo, on looking at the Milky Way through his new telescope in the winter of 1609–1610.

The stars and galaxies lie a very long way away. Even the nearest star, Proxima Centauri, lies more than 25 trillion miles (40 trillion km) from Earth. Light from this star takes more than four years to reach us, which means that it lies more than four light-years away.

Astronomers use the light-year as a unit to measure distances in space. It is the distance a beam of light travels in a year—about 5.9 trillion miles (9.5 trillion km). Some of the most distant objects that astronomers see in the most advanced telescopes lie more than 12 billion light-years away from us.

USING TELESCOPES

On the ground, astronomers use telescopes to gather the light from distant stars and galaxies. Telescopes use lenses or mirrors to gather and focus the light. Telescopes that use lenses are called refractors; telescopes that use mirrors are called reflectors.

Astronomers also use telescopes to study radio waves that stars and galaxies emit. But ground-based instruments cannot study many of the other rays given off by stars and galaxies because Earth's atmosphere partly or completely blocks them. But instruments on satellites, which of course fly high above the atmosphere, can detect these rays.

The atmosphere absorbs gamma rays, X-rays, infrared rays, and microwaves. Along with visible light and radio waves, these rays belong to the electromagnetic spectrum, a family of waves that differ from one another in their wavelength.

▶ *Three dish antennae at Goldstone Deep Space Communication Complex in the Mojave Desert in California. They are used for radio astronomy as well as for communicating with space probes.*

▼ *A radio "picture" of a galaxy. Most radio waves come from the center, or nucleus, of a galaxy.*

ON THE RADIO

A radio telescope looks nothing like an ordinary light telescope. The most common type uses a huge metal dish to gather radio signals and focus them onto an antenna. The signals are then fed to a receiver connected to a computer that displays the signals as an image on a monitor. It produces the image we would see if our eyes were sensitive to radio wavelengths.

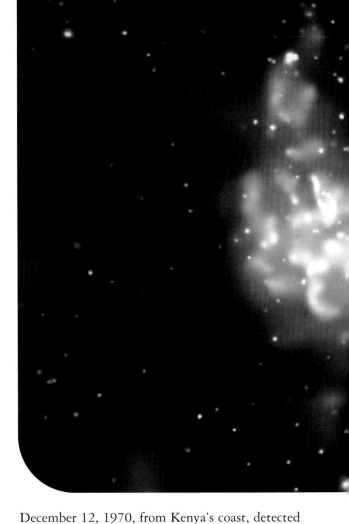

Imagine that an electromagnetic wave is like an ocean wave: A wavelength is the distance between the crest of one wave to the crest of the next wave. Gamma rays have the shortest wavelength (less than one-hundredth of a billionth of a meter); radio waves are the longest—up to a kilometer or more. (Wavelengths always use metric measurements.)

GAMMA RAYS

The first satellites to carry gamma-ray experiments were the OSOs (Orbiting Solar Observatories) launched in the 1960s. In 1969, Vela satellites, designed to detect nuclear tests on the ground, detected intense bursts of gamma radiation from space. The *Compton Gamma Ray Observatory* (1991–2000) and Europe's *Integral Satellite* (launched 2002) studied these gamma-ray bursts in detail.

Gamma-ray "bursters"—the sources of the gamma-ray bursts—proved to be among the most energetic occurrences in the Universe. Astronomers estimate that colliding neutron stars might be one source of these bursters. Neutron stars consist of atomic particles called neutrons packed tightly together. They are incredibly dense—just a teaspoonful of their matter weighs millions of tons.

X-RAYS

Instruments on high-altitude rockets discovered the first X-ray sources in space in the 1960s. In 1971, the satellite *Uhuru* (Swahili for "Freedom"), launched

▼ *Gamma rays are the shortest electromagnetic waves. Then come X-rays, ultraviolet rays, visible light, infrared rays, microwaves, and radio waves.*

December 12, 1970, from Kenya's coast, detected X-rays coming from Cygnus X-1, a source of X-rays in the constellation Cygnus. Astronomers believe that this indicates the presence of a "black hole." A black hole is a region of space with gravity so great that nothing—not even light—escapes from it. It also represents the final stage in the life of a very big star. Later X-ray satellites, such as the *Einstein Observatory* (launched 1978), *Rosat* (1990), and *Chandra* (1999), comprehensively mapped the X-ray sources in the Universe. These data show not only the location of black holes but also of pulsars—spinning neutron stars and supernova remnants—of energy remaining after a big star explodes into a supernova.

| Gamma rays | X-rays | Ultraviolet rays | Visible light |

LITTLE GREEN MEN

Stars that are about three times more massive than our Sun end their life spectacularly by blasting apart in the biggest explosions in the Universe: Supernovas. In a supernova, the core, or center, of the star becomes so dense it finally collapses under it own gravity. Eventually, it shrinks to a body of neutrons squashed together to only about 12 miles (20 km) across. This tiny neutron star spins around rapidly, sending out beams of light or other radiation—much like a celestial lighthouse. If we detect these beams on Earth, we see them as pulses each time they flash past. We now call these bodies pulsars. In 1967, Jocelyn Bell and other British radio astronomers discovered the first pulsars. They briefly called these flashing sources of light LGM, for "Little Green Men," but soon realized that these sources were indeed a new type of space object.

▲ The Chandra X-ray Observatory *captured this X-ray image of a huge explosion. They believe it originated in a massive black hole that we call Sagittarius A at the center of our galaxy,*

▼ *Data returned by IRAS (InfraRed Astronomy Satellite) show a full-galaxy side view at infrared wavelengths.*

INFRARED

Some ground-based telescopes on high mountaintops, such as the Mauna Kea Observatory in Hawaii, can study infrared wavelengths that pass through the atmosphere. But only satellites can observe the full range of infrared wavelengths. The leading satellites have been *IRAS* (*Infrared Astronomy Satellite*, launched 1983),

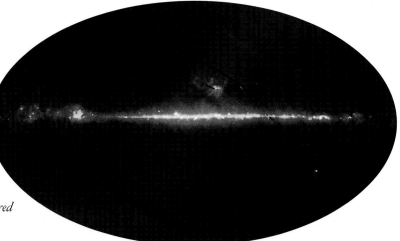

Infrared rays   Microwaves   Radio waves

Europe's *ISO* (*Infrared Space Observatory*, 1995), and NASA's *Spitzer Space Telescope* (formerly the *Space Infrared Telescope Facility*, 2003). Among the infrared sources the satellites detected were vast, cool clouds of matter found among the stars and stellar "nurseries" where new stars are born. The familiar pillars of the Eagle Nebula are among the most famous star nurseries discovered.

MICROWAVES

Space itself gives off weak microwave background radiation—very short radio waves, the same as those used in microwave ovens. The type of radiation given off by anything depends on its temperature. The background radiation given off by space indicates that its temperature averages –454° F (–270° C). Scientists theorize that this is the heat remaining from the "Big Bang" that supposedly created the Universe some 15 billion years ago. Back then, the Universe was very tiny and very hot; it is still expanding and cooling down.

In 1992, the U.S. satellite *COBE* (*Cosmic Background Explorer*) discovered that the background microwave radiation differed by location. Temperature "ripples" in space varied slightly cooler than average. Astronomers estimate that areas like these allowed the formation of the first galaxies in the early Universe.

▼ COBE *view of our galaxy.*

THE *HUBBLE SPACE TELESCOPE*

The *Hubble Space Telescope* (*HST*) produced the greatest scientific returns and captured the imagination of the public. Named after U.S. astronomer Edwin Hubble, who in 1923 proved the existence of independent star systems beyond our own galaxy, the *HST* is an amazing astronomy tool.

The *HST* was launched from the Space Shuttle *Discovery* (*STS-31*) on April 24, 1990. Unfortunately, a manufacturing fault caused its builder to grind the *HST*'s main mirror with the wrong curvature. This caused a blurring of the images sent back by the *HST*. A daring shuttle rescue/repair mission in 1993 corrected the fault.

▲ Hubble Space Telescope *view of the Tarantula Nebula.*

FIXING HUBBLE

NASA's shuttle rescue mission (*STS-61*) to fix *Hubble*'s "flawed vision" occurred in December 1993. Using its robot arm, Space Shuttle *Endeavour* plucked *Hubble* from orbit. Space-walking astronauts made five EVAs (extravehicular activities) to replace equipment on *Hubble*. The most important part replaced was a unit called COSTAR (Corrective Optics Space Telescope Axial Replacement). When fitted, its ten small mirrors corrected the main mirror defect. By the time the rescue mission ended, *Hubble* had perfect vision. A NASA spokesperson remarked, "The patient has a new vision of incredible clarity."

▼ *Astronaut at work repairing the* Hubble Space Telescope.

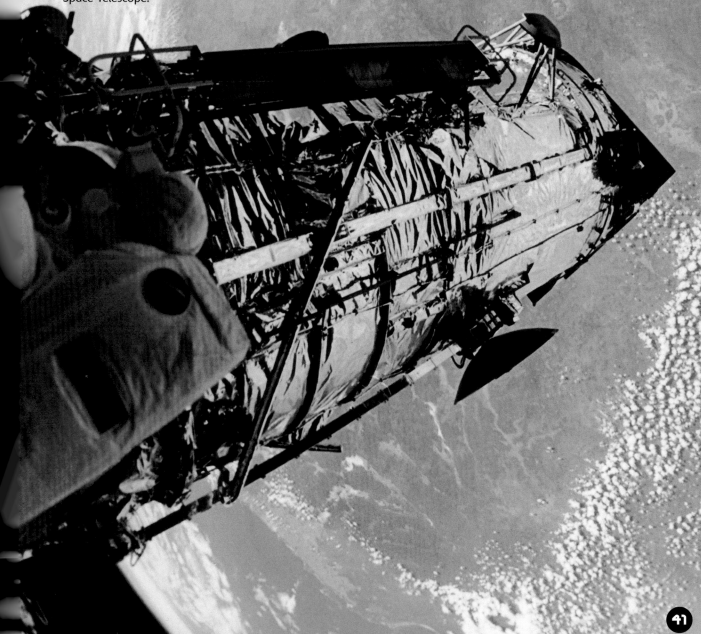

Since then, the *HST* has revealed in glorious color a host of external galaxies as well as a multitude of other celestial objects, such as nebulae, star clusters, neutron stars, and active galaxies such as quasars. Quasi-stellar objects, or quasars, are some of the most intriguing astronomical bodies in the Universe. They resemble stars in the sky, but they actually lie billions of light-years away. Each is hundreds of times brighter than an ordinary galaxy.

HOW THE *HST* WORKS

The *Hubble Space Telescope* is a huge satellite. More than 43 feet (13 m) long and 14 feet (4.3 m) in diameter, the *HST* has a mass of more than 12.5 tons (11.5 tonnes). *Hubble* orbits 50 miles (560 km) above Earth. Two large solar panels provide power, and two antennae are used for communications.

Hubble works like a simple reflecting telescope, with a large, curved primary (first) mirror 98 inches (2.4 m) in diameter. This mirror gathers light and reflects it to a smaller secondary mirror, which in turn reflects it down through a hole in the primary. Light is brought to a focus behind the primary mirror and then directed into various instruments. Most of the original instruments have been replaced on servicing missions in 1993, 1997, 1999, and 2002.

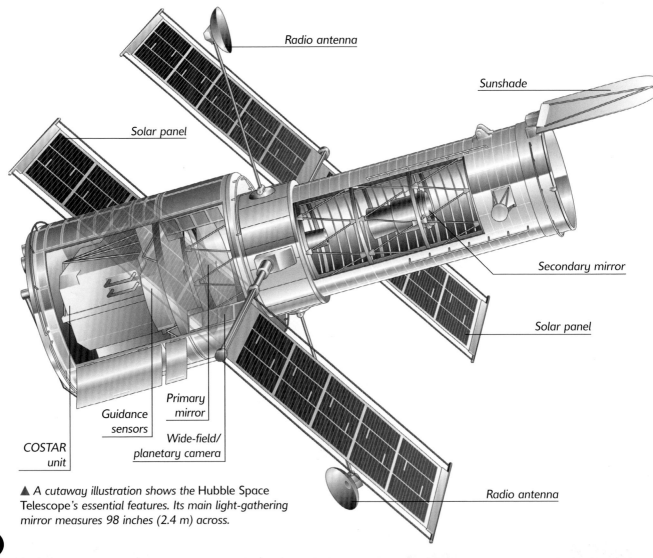

Radio antenna

Sunshade

Solar panel

Secondary mirror

Solar panel

Guidance sensors

Primary mirror

Wide-field/ planetary camera

COSTAR unit

Radio antenna

▲ A cutaway illustration shows the Hubble Space Telescope's essential features. Its main light-gathering mirror measures 98 inches (2.4 m) across.

The most important of *Hubble*'s instruments is the Wide-Field Planetary Camera (WF/PC). It forms images with CCDs (charge-coupled devices), just like the digital cameras we use on Earth. An instrument called NICMOS (Near Infrared Camera and Multi-Object Spectrometer) allows *Hubble* to also see in infrared wavelengths. The ACS (Advanced Camera for Surveys) takes detailed images of galaxies and searches for other planetary systems.

THE *JWST*

Without further servicing missions, the *Hubble Space Telescope* will cease operation in 2008. A replacement for the *HST* should be ready for launch around 2011. It is the *James Webb Space Telescope* (*JWST*), named after James Webb, a former NASA administrator.

The *JWST* will have a much larger light-gathering mirror—about 21 feet (6.5 m)—than the *HST*. Instead of an Earth orbit, the *JWST* will be placed in orbit around the Sun at a point in space about 930,000 miles (1.5 million km) from Earth.

The new telescope will "see" mainly in infrared wavelengths. It will target young stars, young planetary systems, and young galaxies. Astronomers hope the *JWST* will shed light on the dark ages of the Universe, just after the "Big Bang," when stars and galaxies first began to form.

VERY LARGE TELESCOPES

The latest generation of large, ground-based telescopes are beginning to send back images that rival those of *Hubble*. The *Very Large Telescope* (*VLT*), located at the European Southern Observatory in Chile, uses four reflectors, each with a mirror 27 feet (8.2 m) across. With the telescopes linked together by computer, the *VLT* can produce incredibly detailed images: Astronomers claim they could spot an astronaut walking on the Moon.

▼ The Hubble Space Telescope *returns to orbit after the servicing mission in March 2002. In January 2004, NASA announced that—because of the* Columbia *accident—it would risk no more missions to repair or service* Hubble.

1957

October 4: The Space Age begins when the Soviet Union launches *Sputnik*.

November 3: *Sputnik 2* is launched carrying space dog Laika.

1959

January: The Soviet probe *Luna 1* flies past the Moon at a distance of about 3,000 miles (5,000 km), becoming the first object to escape Earth's gravity.

September: *Luna 2* crash-lands on the Moon near the crater Archimedes, becoming the first man-made object to reach another world.

October: *Luna 3* flies past the Moon—taking the very first pictures of the Moon's far side that we cannot see from Earth.

1960

March: The U.S. probe *Pioneer 5* becomes the first deep-space probe, transmitting data at distances up to 23 million miles (37 million km).

1962

December: The U.S. *Mariner 2* probe flies within 22,000 miles (35,000 km) of Venus, reporting on conditions there.

1965

July 15: *Mariner 4* transmits the first close-up photographs of Mars, approaching as close as 6,000 miles (9,600 km).

July 31: *Ranger 7* becomes the first successful U.S. lunar probe, transmitting close-up pictures of the Moon before crash-landing.

1966

January: *Luna 9* lands an instrument capsule on the Moon.

April: *Luna 10* goes into lunar orbit.

May: NASA's *Surveyor 1* lands on the Moon.

August: NASA's *Lunar Orbiter 1* enters lunar orbit.

1967

October: The Soviet probe *Venera 4* releases a capsule into Venus's atmosphere.

1971

November: NASA's *Mariner 9* becomes the first successful Mars orbiter, returning more than 7,000 pictures.

1973

December: NASA's *Pioneer 10* (launched March 1972) flies past Jupiter, becoming the first probe to reach the giant planet.

1974

February: *Mariner 10* flies via Venus to Mercury, making passes of that planet in March and September, and also in March 1975.

1975

October: Soviet probes *Venera*s 9 and *10* land capsules on Venus; they take the first close-up pictures of the planet.

1976

June and August: NASA's *Viking 1* and *Viking 2* go into orbit around Mars. Their landers touch down on the surface in July and September.

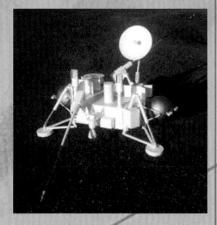

1978

In December, NASA's *Pioneer-Venus 1* begins imaging Venus's surface using radar.

1979

March: NASA's *Voyager 1* (launched September 1977) reports back from Jupiter; *Voyager 2* (launched August 1977), in July.

August: NASA's *Pioneer-Saturn* (formerly *Pioneer 11*, launched April 1973) returns close-up pictures of Saturn.

1980

November: *Voyager 1* flies past Saturn.

1985

June: An international probe, *VEGA 1,* flies past Venus, dropping off a lander on its way to Halley's comet.

1986

January: *Voyager 2* encounters Uranus.

March: The European Space Agency's *Giotto* probe takes the first photographs of the nucleus of Halley's comet.

1989

August: *Voyager 2* flies past Neptune.

1990

April: *Hubble Space Telescope* is launched from *Space Shuttle Discovery*.

September: NASA's *Magellan* probe begins mapping the surface of Venus with radar.

1991

October: NASA's *Galileo* sends back the first images of an asteroid (Gaspra).

1995

December: *Galileo* goes into orbit around Jupiter.

2000

February: *NEAR-Shoemaker* goes into orbit around asteroid Eros, landing on it a year later.

2004

January: ESA's *Mars Express* begins returning the best pictures yet of Mars from orbit. In the same month, NASA's Mars rovers *Spirit* and *Opportunity* begin roaming the Martian surface. NASA's *Stardust* collects dust from comet Wild-2.

July: NASA's *Cassini-Huygens* enters orbit around Saturn; it later releases probe to land on Titan.

2006

January: *Stardust* scheduled to return samples of comet dust to Earth.

2011

James Webb Space Telescope, the replacement for the *Hubble Space Telescope*, scheduled for launch around this time.

2014

ESA *Rosetta* probe scheduled to encounter comet Churyumov-Gerasimenko and land a probe on its surface.

asteroids
A group of small bodies that circles the Sun, mainly between the orbits of Mars and Jupiter.

axis
An imaginary line around which a body spins.

comet
An icy body that circles the Sun and becomes visible to us when solar radiation causes it to release clouds of gas and dust.

crater
A pit dug out of the surface of a planet or moon by the impact of a meteorite or asteroid.

EVA (ExtraVehicular Acitivity)
Leaving a spacecraft to perform work in space; also called space walking.

fly-by
When a spacecraft flies past a planet without going into orbit around it or landing.

gas giant
One of the giant outer planets—Jupiter, Saturn, Uranus, and Neptune—that consist mainly of gas and liquid gas.

gravity-assist
Using the gravitational pull of one planet to "slingshot," or redirect and accelerate, a spacecraft toward another planet or body.

meteorite
A space rock that impacts a planet or moon.

moon
A natural satellite of a planet.

orbit
The path in space taken by one body circling another, such as a planet circling the Sun.

orbiter
A spacecraft that goes into orbit around a planet.

planet
A large celestial object that circles a central star; it emits no light of its own and may have moons.

probe
A spacecraft sent to explore another planet, moon, asteroid, comet, or other celestial object.

radiation
Electromagnetic rays of differing wavelengths of energy emitted by stars and other celestial objects in the Universe.

retrorocket
A smaller rocket fired to slow down a spacecraft. Retrorockets are often used to decrease a spacecraft's speed for a safe landing.

ring
Chunks of ice and rock torn apart by a planet's gravity in orbit around that planet; Saturn has the most prominent rings in our Solar System.

rocket
A self-contained engine that burns fuel in oxygen to produce a stream of hot gases. As the gases shoot out backward through a nozzle, the rocket is propelled forward, by reaction. Rockets can work in space because they carry their own oxygen supply.

rover
A small vehicle landed on a planet to explore the surface.

satellite
A small body that circles a larger one in space. Most of the planets in our Solar System have natural satellites, or moons. Earth also has thousands of artificial satellites—man-made spacecraft that have been launched into orbit.

shepherd moon
A small moon that orbits close to a planet's rings and helps keep objects in the ring in place.

solar cell
A device that produces electricity by harnessing the energy in sunlight.

Solar System
Our Sun and its family of planets, moons, asteroids, and comets.

terrestrial planet
One of the Earthlike, rocky planets—Mercury, Venus, or Mars.

trajectory
The path of a spacecraft through space.

BOOKS TO READ

Benson, Michael. **Beyond: Visions of the Interplanetary Probes**. Abrams, 2003.

Bredeson, Carmen. **NASA Planetary Spacecraft: Galileo, Magellan, Pathfinder, and Voyager**. Enslow Publishers, 2000.

Cattemole, Peter. **Atlas of Venus**. Cambridge University Press, 1997.

Cole, Michael. **Galileo Spacecraft: Mission to Jupiter**. Enslow Publishers, 1999.
Croswell, Ken. **Magnificent Mars**.The Free Press, 2003.

Hartmann, William. **Traveler's Guide to Mars**. Workman Publishing, 2003.

Kerrod, Robin. **Hubble—The Mirror on the Universe**. Firefly Books, 2003.

Kerrod, Robin. **The Journeys of Voyager**. Prion, 1990.

Mishkin, Andrew. **Sojourner: An Insider's View of the Mars Pathfinder Mission**. Berkley Hardcover, 2003.

Raeburn, Paul. **Mars: Uncovering the Secrets of the Red Planet**. National Geographic, 1998.

PLACES TO VISIT

Most U.S. space probes are launched from Cape Canaveral Air Force Station in Florida. Several Space Shuttle missions also launched probes from Earth orbit. The shuttle fleet takes off from the Kennedy Space Center on Merritt Island, just inland from Cape Canaveral.

Guided bus tours of the launch facilities at the Kennedy Space Center and the Cape Canaveral Air Force Station occur daily. For details of upcoming events, check out the following web sites: www.nasa.gov/; www.ksc.nasa.gov/; and www.pao.ksc.nasa.gov/kscpao/schedule/schedule.htm.

The Johnson Space Center in Houston, Texas, has a visitors' center and rocket park. It is also home base for U.S. astronauts. For further details, see www.jsc.nasa.gov/ and http://spacecenter.org/.

Many other air and space museums around the United States offer exciting space exhibits:

International Women's Air and Space Museum, Cleveland, OH www.iwasm.org/

Intrepid Sea-Air-Space Museum, New York City www.intrepidmuseum.org/

Neil Armstrong Air and Space Museum, Wapakoneta, OH www.ohiohistory.org/places/armstron/

Oregon Air and Space Museum, Eugene, OR www.oasm.org/

Pima Air and Space Museum, Tucson, AZ www.pimaair.org/

San Diego Aerospace Museum, San Diego, CA www.aerospacemuseum.org/

The Smithsonian National Air and Space Museum (**NASM**), Washington, D.C. See the largest collection of historic air and spacecraft in the world. Exhibits include rockets and spacecraft such as Mercury, Gemini, and Apollo. For more details and opening times, visit the NASM web site: www.nasm.edu/

U.S. Space and Rocket Center, Huntsville, AL www.ussrc.com

Virginia Air and Space Center, Hampton, VA www.vasc.org/

SPACE CAMPS

Florida, Alabama, and other locations host a number of space camps in the summer months. Lessons include learning about the nature and problems of spaceflight as well as "hands-on" experience in spaceflight simulators.
www.spacecamp.com
www.vaspaceflightacademy.org

WEB SITES

Hubble—View a gallery of celestial images and more. http://hubblesite.org/

NASA History—NASA's history office includes original documents, sound clips, and footage. http://history.nasa.gov/

NASA Kids—Information, games, and activities. http://kids.msfc.nasa.gov/

Pioneers 10 and 11 Facts, details, links to other sites. www.aerospaceguide.net/pioneer10.html

SOHO—The latest information on solar research. http://umbra.nascom.nasa.gov/images/latest.html

Space.com—Up-to-the-minute news about space exploration. www.space.com

Voyagers An overview of probe missions. http://home.cwru.edu/~sjr16/20th_far_voyagers.html

ABOUT THE AUTHOR
Robin Kerrod writes on space and astronomy for a wide audience. In such best-selling titles as *Hubble, Apollo, Voyager,* and *Illustrated History of NASA,* he has chronicled man's exciting assault on the space frontier. Robin is a former winner of Britain's prestigious COPUS science book prize.